★ POP CULTURE BIOS

MAIA
MITCHELL

TALENT FROM DOWN UNDER

HEATHER E. SCHWARTZ

Lerner Publications Company
A division of Lerner Publishing Group, Inc.
241 First Avenue North
Minneapolis, MN 55401 USA

For reading levels and more information, look up this title at
www.lernerbooks.com.

Library of Congress Cataloging-in-Publication Data

Schwartz, Heather E.
    Maia Mitchell : talent from down under / by Heather E.
Schwartz.
        pages cm. — (Pop culture bios)
    Includes index.
    ISBN 978–1–4677–3672–5 (lib. bdg. : alk. paper)
    ISBN 978–1–4677–4733–2 (eBook)
    1. Mitchell, Maia—Juvenile literature 2. Actors—Australia—
Biography—Juvenile literature. 3. Singers—Australia—
Biography—Juvenile literature. I. Title.
PN3018.M58S39 2015
791.4302'8092—dc23 [B]   2014001660

Manufactured in the United States of America
1 – PC – 7/15/14

INTRODUCTION

Maia (LEFT) poses with Cierra Ramirez (RIGHT), her costar on *The Fosters*.

One day in 2013, Maia Mitchell was hanging out in her living room. Dressed in sweats and surrounded by family, she couldn't have been more comfy. They were all just chatting when Maia got a big surprise. The stunning, stylish, and talented superstar Jennifer Lopez entered the room.

Maia wasn't chilling at her own home that day. She was working. The living room was the set of her new TV show, *The Fosters*. The clothes were her costume. And her family was actually a family of cast members. The show wasn't on the air yet, but the cast had been working together for a while, and they'd grown close.

Maia acting in *The Fosters*

Just three years earlier, Maia had been living in Australia, hoping to land some new acting gigs. Since 2011, her life had changed dramatically. The past three years had been a whirlwind of luck and opportunity.

Maia poses at a charity event in 2014.

Now, Maia was one of the main characters in an American TV show. JLo, one of Hollywood's biggest celebrities, was the show's executive producer. People were definitely going to pay attention to *The Fosters*. This was a career-making moment for Maia. And really, her career had only just begun.

Maia (BOTTOM LEFT) poses with executive producer Jennifer Lopez (BOTTOM CENTER) and cast members of *The Fosters*.

CHAPTER ONE
AUSSIE ACTRESS

Maia grew up in Lismore, a town in New South Wales, Australia.

Maia was born on August 18, 1993, and grew up in Lismore, Australia. She didn't spend much time in movie theaters as a kid. She wasn't glued to the TV either—her parents wouldn't allow it. But she always loved the idea of getting into show business and becoming a performer.

Instead of watching *others* perform, Maia spent her time learning how to perform herself. She took dance classes and learned to play the guitar. She took theater classes too, and she won roles in plays at school and in community theater.

WORD PROBLEM

Maia had trouble saying the word cucumber when she was little. She's told the media the problem went on until she was seven!

Maia poses with a guitar in 2013.

Small-Screen Star

When Maia was twelve, she got the chance to take her talents to the next level. She auditioned for the Australian TV series *Mortified*, about a young girl who was constantly embarrassed by her family. After her audition, Maia was the one mortified. "I left the audition crying, thinking it was horrible," she recalled in an interview.

But it couldn't have been *too* bad—she wound up landing a major role in the show. Throughout Australia, Maia became known by the name of her character: Brittany Flune. She played the pretty neighbor of the show's main character.

Maia (LEFT) and costar Marny Kennedy (RIGHT) on the set of *Mortified*

SCHOOL DAYS

Maia's favorite subjects in school were drama and English.

In 2007, *Mortified* ended. But Maia's career kept on going. Her next role was on the Australian series *Trapped*. The show was about a group of kids trying to survive at a dangerous scientific research base after their parents disappear. In 2008 and 2009, Maia played Natasha Hamilton in twenty-five episodes. When *Trapped* ended, she played her same character in the show's sequel, *Castaway*, in 2010 and 2011.

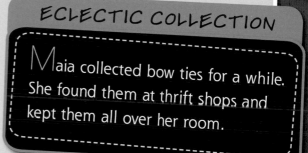
American Audition

In 2011, Maia decided to leave home and settle in Sydney, Australia, to continue her acting career. But there was one catch. Her management team in the United States thought she'd be perfect for an American film. On the day she moved, her team begged her to audition. Maia agreed to give it a chance.

SEQUEL =
a show that continues the story where another show left off

The process wasn't easy, though. Maia started off by auditioning from Australia. The movie producers sent her scenes to act out. She recorded herself and sent the recordings back. But it was hard to know how to really shine. Maia did not have the whole script. So she didn't know everything about her character. She had to guess at how to play her.

AUSSIE ACCENT, OC ACCENT

While living in Australia, Maia perfected her American accent by watching TV. Her favorite show was *The OC*.

The OC cast smiles for the camera at the Billboard Music Awards in 2003.

Maia answers to many nicknames. People call her My-My, Australia, and Mitch.

American Auditions Take Two

Next, producers wanted to Skype with Maia. But the time difference created awkward delays, and technical difficulties also arose. A lot of the time, she had to shout to be heard. And they *still* couldn't hear her! Finally, the producers flew Maia to the States so they could meet her in person.

It was a big trip for Maia, and she did it alone. Arriving in the States, she went straight from the hours-long plane ride to her big audition. She had to show the producers she could sing, dance, and act. She had the skills to score the role. But feeling the jet lag setting in, Maia didn't think her chances were good.

CHAPTER TWO

TEEN BEACH BREAKOUT

Cast members from *Teen Beach Movie* have fun on set.

After her many auditions, Maia was surprised to learn she'd been chosen to play the female lead in the Disney Channel's *Teen Beach Movie*. She was even more shocked after she learned she'd beaten out thousands of girls for the part. When reporters asked her why she thought she was picked, Maia could only guess. **"I didn't think I had a chance at it. It's kind of humbling,"** she said. "I didn't dress up for the auditions. I kind of went in and was myself and I've always done that." It must have been exactly what the directors were looking for.

Maia strikes a pose at a Teen Beach Movie screening in London in 2013.

In *Teen Beach Movie*, Maia would play McKenzie, a teen whose life is transformed when she's magically transported into a 1960s beach movie. Suddenly, her own life was headed in an unexpected direction too. She wasn't going to settle in Sydney as she'd originally planned. At eighteen years old, she moved to Los Angeles, California.

And she started feeling the pressure. As a lead in the movie (with Ross Lynch as her costar), Maia knew the worst that could happen if she didn't pull off an amazing performance. The entire movie could tank!

SINGING STAR

Maia sang about ten songs for her *Teen Beach Movie* auditions. One was Jessie J's "Price Tag." She also sang songs by Adele and Train.

Maia and Ross Lynch

Debby Ryan, star of the Disney show *Jessie*, was one of Maia's first friends when she moved to the States. Maia even had a guest spot on the show in 2013.

Maia learned to surf for her role in the movie.

Surf's Up!

With Maia at work, though, there was zero chance of that. Right away, she started prepping for her role. One of the first things on the list was pretty nerve-racking. She had to learn to surf.

Before she could even get up on a board, Maia needed more muscle. She worked with a personal trainer to build upper body strength. She also worked with a surf trainer and practiced every day for a month. Setting her jitters aside, she learned to ride the waves.

On set, the challenges kept coming. Maia learned to sing all kinds of music, from surf rock and Motown R & B to pop and rockabilly, a rock and country combo. She recorded music in a studio for the very first time. She also stepped up her moves to dance alongside professional dancers.

STICKY STYLE

While filming *Teen Beach Movie*, Maia had her hair styled into a beehive. One day, she forgot her hair was so tall. She snagged her hair in a tree and got stuck!

Loving Every Minute

Maia really enjoyed the acting part of filming, but nailing down a favorite moment was tough. Maia told reporters how much she loved the energy on set and the location, a beautiful beach in Puerto Rico. She said it was fun wearing crazy costumes, such as a vintage 1960s swimsuit and a biker outfit. And she liked singing, dancing, and acting all at once.

Working with her fellow cast members made the entire experience unforgettable. They were constantly pranking one another. Some of the cast hid another cast member's clothes in the microwave, so he couldn't change out of his costume for a while. Another was caught by surprise when she found a live iguana in her trailer!

Small-Town Superstar

When the movie aired in the United States in July 2013, more than 8 million viewers tuned in to watch. In August, *Teen Beach Movie* premiered in Australia. It was an event that had Maia walking a yellow carpet and having her picture taken by the media. She was back—and she was big news. The small-town Aussie girl was now a movie star!

MAIA ON MUSIC

Maia loves playing guitar and writing music. But she's not pursuing music as a career. For now, it's a fun hobby for her to enjoy during her downtime.

Maia and Ross Lynch take the stage during the 2013 Teen Choice Awards.

CHAPTER THREE

FORWARD FOCUS

Maia at the *Teen Beach Movie* screening in California in 2013

Teen Beach Movie made Maia famous. But she still had to audition for her next role. She was visiting Australia when she got the script for the TV show *The Fosters*. She loved it. She flew back to L.A. to audition and screen-test for a part on the show.

SCREEN-TEST =
to audition for a show or movie through a recording

Maia hugs Hayden Byerly, a costar on *The Fosters*.

At first, things didn't look good. During the test, she flubbed her lines. But the producers gave her a second chance, and this time, she nailed it. Later, she said she was glad executive producer Jennifer Lopez wasn't there to see her screw up. That would have been *really* nerve-racking!

ROLE MODELS

Maia would love to work with Meryl Streep. Her other acting idols include Natalie Portman, Amy Adams, and Jennifer Lawrence.

Research and Development

In *The Fosters*, Maia had the role of Callie, a foster child living in a nontraditional family. Maia's TV fam included two moms and other foster kids, adopted kids, and biological children too. Being part of such a complex cast would be challenging work, but Maia was psyched to do her best with it. It would give her a chance to show what she could do as an actress. Some of her talent came naturally. But she was dedicated to developing her acting abilities too.

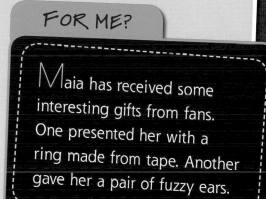

FOR ME?

Maia has received some interesting gifts from fans. One presented her with a ring made from tape. Another gave her a pair of fuzzy ears.

Maia hangs with *The Fosters* cast members in 2013.

Maia chills with David Lambert (CENTER) and Cierra Ramirez (RIGHT) on the set of The Fosters.

To research her role, she met foster kids. She learned their stories, and through her character, she tried to express how they felt. She told the media she had a family member who had spent time in foster care. The personal link helped her feel a special bond with foster kids and a connection with her role.

Maia worked twelve to fifteen hours a day on *The Fosters*. She was proud to be part of such a groundbreaking show, and all the hard work was worth it. "It's really cool to be part of a show that is quite progressive," she said in an interview.

PROGRESSIVE =
forward-thinking and often groundbreaking

Maia laughs with costars Hayden Byerly (CENTER) and David Lambert (RIGHT).

Focus on the Future

Since *Teen Beach Movie*, Maia's acting career was on fast-forward. On the set of *The Fosters*, she learned more about other aspects of the entertainment industry too. She started working closely with the directors of *The Fosters* to learn the ins and outs of their job. And she started dreaming of the future.

STRESS-FREE STYLE

Maia glams it up for Hollywood events. But jeans and Converse sneakers are staples in her everyday wardrobe.

Maia takes a photo with a fan during the *Teen Beach Movie* premiere in Australia in 2013.

She developed new career goals. She decided she wanted to write, produce, and direct her own movies one day. She also began thinking it might be fun to run her own production company in her home country of Australia. Maia knows she can't expect to just snap her fingers and reach these goals. They will take time and a lot of hard work. But Maia feels ready. After all, the talent from down under is always up for a challenge!

PRODUCE = to organize and oversee the creation of a show or movie

MAIA PICS!

Maia with some of the cast of *Teen Beach Movie*

Maia and Cierra Ramirez

SOURCE NOTES

10 "Maia Mitchell in Disney's 'Teen Beach Musical'—Interview on Ch 9 'Mornings' Show," YouTube video, 1:40, posted by HarryManCam, May 11, 2012, https://www.youtube.com/watch?v=n_B6YUvYJ50.

15 Ibid.

25 "Behind the Scenes of 'The Fosters' Cambio Interview," YouTube video, 0:14, posted by Cambio, June 11, 2013, https://www.youtube.com/watch?v=qM1gZzCMJBQ.

MORE MAIA INFO

ABC Family—*The Fosters*
http://abcfamily.go.com/shows/the-fosters/cast/callie
Get the facts on Maia and her character on *The Fosters*.

Maia's Facebook Page
https://www.facebook.com/pages/Maia-Mitchell/166485506806723
If you're a Facebook user, form a Facebook friendship with your fav Aussie star.

Maia's Instagram Page
http://instagram.com/maiamitch#
See for yourself what Maia's been up to.

Maia's Twitter Page
https://twitter.com/MaiaMitchell
Keep tabs on Maia's everyday thoughts.

Schwartz, Heather E. *Ross Lynch: Actor, Singer, Dancer, Superstar.* Minneapolis: Lerner Publications, 2015. Read up on Maia's *Teen Beach Movie* costar.

"This Is Who I Am with Maia Mitchell"
https://www.youtube.com/watch?v=kbEm3V-ToBo
In this video, Maia gushes about Australia; strums her guitar; and dotes on her little brother, Charlie.

The images in this book are used with the permission of: © Joe Kohen/Getty Images, pp. 2, 14 (top left); © FeatureFlash/Shutterstock.com, pp. 3 (bottom), 15, 21; © Frazer Harrison/AMA2013/FilmMagic/Getty Images, p. 4 (bottom); © Jon Kopaloff/FilmMagic/Getty Images, p. 4 (top left), 28 (left); © Don Arnold/WireImage/Getty Images, p. 4 (top right); © Tony Rivetti/ABC FAMILY/Getty Images, p. 5, 23; © David Livingston/Getty Images, p. 6; AP Photo/ABC Family, Bob D'Amico, p. 7, 14, 18; © Michael Bezjian/Getty Images, p. 8 (top); © Petpics/Alamy, p. 8 (bottom); © Araya Diaz/AMA2013/Getty Images, p. 9; © Juno Searle/Newspix/Getty Images, p. 10; © Carlo Allegri/Getty Images, p. 12; AP Photo/Chris Pizello/Invision, p. 13; AP Photo/Disney Channel, Francisco Roman, p. 14 (bottom); © Rodrigo Vaz/FilmMagic/Getty Images, p. 16; © Francisco Roman/Disney Channel/Getty Images, p. 17; © Kevin Winter/Getty Images, p. 20 (top); © Helga Esteb/Shutterstock.com, pp. 20 (bottom left), 22, 29 (top middle); AP Photo/Richard Shotwell/Invision, pp. 20 (bottom right), 28 (bottom); © Eric McCandleless/ABC Family/Getty Images, p. 24; AP Photo/Paul A. Herbert/Invision, p. 25; © Joe Seer/Shutterstock.com, p. 26; © Don Arnold/WireImage/Getty Images, p. 27; AP Photo/Diana Gomez/Rex Features, p. 28 (top left); © Paul Morigi/WireImage/Getty Images, p. 29 (bottom left); © s_buckley/Shutterstock.com, p. 29 (right and top left).

Front Cover: © Jon Kopaloff/FilmMagic/Getty Images, (large image); © D. Long/Globe Photos Inc./ImageCollect, (inset).

Back Cover: © Helga Esteb/Shutterstock.com.

Main body text set in Shannon Std Book 12/18.
Typeface provided by Monotype Typography.